FINDING
GENUINE
PRACTICE

THE EIGHT VERSES OF TRAINING THE MIND

AS TAUGHT BY
THE KARMAPA, OGYEN TRINLEY DORJE

Translated by Khenpo David Karma Choephel

KTD Publications
Woodstock New York USA

CONTENTS

Preface:
The Karmapa, Ogyen Trinley Dorje

It was Jowo Atisha who brought these mind training practices from India to Tibet. Initially, they were secret and taught to very few people. They were regarded as a high-level practice for experienced practitioners, as not everyone was capable of practicing them. They demanded great courage, determination, and dedication. Geshe Langri Thangpa's *Eight Verses of Training the Mind* was probably the first mind training practice that was opened more widely to the public. The renowned

Kadampa master Geshe Chekawa, who composed the famous *Seven-Point Mind Training*, first began to follow the Kadampa teachings having heard Langri Thangpa's *Eight Verses*. These teachings have been preserved in the Kagyu tradition through the work of Lord Gampopa. He studied both the Kadampa teachings and the Mahamudra tradition and skillfully melded them together into the Dagpo Kagyu. Mind training was an essential part of Kagyu practices from the beginning.

Geshe Langri Thangpa is himself a great example of a genuine, mind-training practitioner. Lojong was the main focus of his whole life; he lived mind training every moment. Because he was always focused on his practice, he rarely smiled, and people nicknamed him "grim-faced" Langri Thangpa. On only one or two rare occasions, was he known to smile. Once, there was a turquoise gemstone on the mandala plate. A little mouse, attracted by the turquoise, scrambled over to the plate and tried to steal it. But it was too heavy, so the mouse called another mouse to help him. Together, one mouse pulled at the stone, and the other mouse pushed; as he watched their efforts, Langri Thangpa smiled.

His practice was so effective that those around him witnessed how even the birds and animals at his monastery refrained from harming each other. A story relates that after he passed away, the next day, an old lady came to Langthang monastery. On the way, she was shocked to see an eagle attacking a smaller bird. When she reached the monastery, she told the monks what she had seen, and declared, "I think Langri Thangpa must have passed away because this never used to happen."

When we talk about *lojong* or "mind training," the *lo* or "mind" referred to is *bodhicitta* the "mind of enlightenment," so primarily mind training means training in bodhicitta. The *Eight Verses* contains all the mind training practices divided into eight stages that can be further divided into two parts: relative truth and absolute truth. The first seven stanzas are instructions on generating relative bodhicitta, and the last stanza concerns absolute bodhicitta. Some people recite the *Eight Verses* only as a prayer or aspiration, but that was not Geshe Langri Thangpa's intention. He envisioned the text being used as a handbook for the practice of mind training. In these verses, he tells us precisely what we have to do.

Through them, he teaches us how to visualize, how to prepare our mind, how to focus, and how to analyze. They cover all the crucial points for taming one's mind and developing bodhicitta. They are not just something to be understood intellectually or paid lip-service; they have to be put into practice.

A parallel example would be training to run a marathon. If we want to get fit, we have to follow a daily exercise program. It requires courage, hard work, and perseverance. Mind training should be like that too. It should be practiced assiduously on a daily basis, and we need to create momentum by planning ahead. In the morning, when we wake up, we should consciously set out a plan of what we will do with our mind throughout the day. In the evening, we should reflect on our thoughts and actions during the day that has passed and assess how successfully we kept to our plan.

Langri Thangpa practiced what he taught. In the *Eight Verses*, it says, "I will take defeat on myself, and give the victory to others." One day, while he was teaching the monks in his monastery, a woman arrived with a baby. "This is your child. I can't take care of it anymore," she exclaimed, thrust it at him, and walked off. He calmly picked up the baby and carried him until he found a wet nurse. He left the baby with her and paid her to raise the child. This incident created a huge scandal and much gossip directed against Langri Thangpa, but he said nothing. And so the baby grew up under his protection. Years later, the woman returned to the monastery with her family and told her story. All her previous children had died, so when this child was born, the family had done a *mo* — a "divination." It said that the only way to save the baby was to give him away to a qualified master. Now the boy had grown up, and they were full of gratitude to Langri Thangpa.

Genuine dharma practice is not separate from life. Generally, when everything is going well, when there are no problems or difficulties, anyone can appear to be a good dharma practitioner. However, when things go wrong, when adversity strikes, that is the real test of our dharma practice.

Finally, I would like to take this opportunity to thank everyone who has worked on the preparation of this book for publication. I hope that it will be of benefit.

17th Karmapa Ogyen Trinley Dorje
June 21, 2020

Introduction

The Gyalwang Karmapa has taught Geshe Langri Thangpa's *Eight Verses of Training the Mind* on several occasions. Though short, this text gets to the core of Mahayana practice, and each time he teaches it, he emphasizes different themes. In this particular teaching, he stressed how we need to bring our practice to bear on the difficulties that face us in our life and our dharma practice — an issue that all practitioners must face if their practice is to be effective.

The teachings in this were originally given in a weekend teaching called "The Art of Happiness" organized by the Foundation for Universal Responsibility of His Holiness the Dalai Lama (FURHHDL) in November 2014. We would also like to thank Rajiv Mehrotra and everyone at FURHHDL for organizing the teaching and their support.

THE EIGHT VERSES OF
TRAINING THE MIND

By thinking of all sentient beings
As more precious than a wish-
  fulfilling.jewel
For accomplishing the highest aim,
I will always hold them dear.

Whenever I'm in the company of others,
I will regard myself as the lowest
  among all,
And from the depths of my heart
Cherish others as supreme.

In my every action, I will watch my mind,

And the moment destructive
  emotions arise,
I will confront them strongly and
  avert them,
Since they will hurt both me and others.

Whenever I see ill-natured beings,
Or those overwhelmed by heavy
  misdeeds or suffering,
I will cherish them as something rare,
As though I'd found a priceless treasure.

Whenever someone out of envy
Does me wrong by attacking or
  belittling me,
I will take defeat on myself,
And give the victory to others.

Even when someone I have helped,
Or in whom I have placed great hopes

Mistreats me very unjustly,
I will view that person as a true
    spiritual teacher.

In brief, directly or indirectly,
I will offer help and happiness to all my
  mothers,
And secretly take on myself
All their hurt and suffering.

I will learn to keep all these practices
Untainted by thoughts of the eight
  worldly concerns.
May I recognize all things as like illusions,
And, without attachment, gain freedom
    from bondage.

*Thus spoke the spiritual master Lang Thang
Dorje Senge. This is completed.
Sarva Mangalam.*

FINDING GENUINE PRACTICE

The topic for these two days of teachings is the *Eight Verses of Training the Mind* by the great Kadampa spiritual master Geshe Langri Thanga Dorje Senge. Mind training is an important practice of the Kadampa school. When we say "mind," we primarily mean bodhicitta, so this is training in bodhicitta. Bodhicitta is not something that everyone is immediately and directly ready to practice and actualize. Instead, we need to train in it gradually and improve it step by step. Thus when we say mind training, we primarily mean training in bodhicitta.

The Hinayana or Foundation vehicle and the Mahayana or Great vehicle are also called "yanas." Sometimes we use the word *yana* to refer to pack animals such as goats, donkeys, or oxen. The reason for this is that they carry packs, hence they can also be called "vehicles." However, there is a difference in the size of the burden that they can carry. For example, goats, which were once used as pack animals, can only carry a very small amount. In comparison, donkeys or oxen can carry much more, and elephants can carry huge loads. Likewise the distinction between the Foundation and Mahayana vehicles, is the size of the load — how much responsibility — they can bear. Some people are only able to carry their own loads; some are able to bear the burden of many people's loads and responsibilities. So that is the distinction between the Foundation and the Mahayana: the amount of responsibility and the size of the burden one is able to bear.

With regard to the Foundation and Mahayana vehicles, it's not just a question of making the aspiration verbally with our mouths, "May all sentient beings be happy; May all sentient beings be free of suffering," it's not merely the words. Rather, it is a question of our heart. How do we feel in our heart? Are we able to bear the burden of treasuring all sentient beings? Do we have the courage to do this? This is what the aspiration is dependent on.

But as I said before, in order to develop the courage to carry the burden or responsibility of the Mahayana, we need to train ourselves in it and increase our training. Merely reciting the Mahayana practices does not make us a Mahayana practitioner. In order to become a Mahayana practitioner, we must also practice the other vehicles. We must do the practices that are in common with the other vehicles and those practices must precede the Mahayana. And so it is only when we have achieved a degree or level of the common dharma practices that we will be able to reach the level of the Mahayana.

For example, there is the text that we are about to discuss here, the *Eight Verses of Training the Mind*. If I were to ask you, is this a Foundation vehicle text or is it a Mahayana text, I think all of you would say that it is a Mahayana text.

And so, if we are studying a Mahayana text, does that mean we are actually studying and practicing the Mahayana dharma? We would have to say we are not sure.

When we are studying the Mahayana dharma, it does not mean that we are definitely doing it as Mahayana dharma practice. The reason is that it depends on our intention. If we do not have the authentic motivation required of the Mahayana dharma, even though we may be studying the mind training texts of the Mahayana, it does not necessarily become the Mahayana dharma for us. So we might point to a text and say, "This is a Mahayana text, or this is a Foundation text." Or, we might see a practitioner and say, "That person is practicing the Mahayana dharma, so they must be a Mahayana practitioner." This is a mistake. Actually, we need to see what our own motivation is and how we ourselves are training. We must direct our attention inwards.

We don't need to point the finger outwards, but instead examine ourselves, inwardly.

In that way, when we talk about training the mind, we mean we are improving our own mind, seeing whether we have been able to focus inwards and tame and pacify our own wild way of being. That is what is important.

ONE: HOLD ALL BEINGS DEAR

By thinking of all sentient beings
As more precious than a wish-
fulfilling jewel
For accomplishing the highest aim,
I will always hold them dear.

It took me a long time to figure out what is meant here by "wish-fulfilling jewel" and the best way to explain it. The wish-fulfilling jewel is a jewel found in the ocean. It is extremely difficult to obtain. You have to go on a long ocean voyage to get it from the King of the Nagas. According to the myth, once you do find this jewel and pray and make offerings to it, it will fulfill all of your desires. It was very difficult for me to think of what we could replace it with.

I thought about it from many perspectives, and then it finally occurred to me that often these days we think of money as similar to a wish-fulfilling jewel, because if you have money you can fulfill your desires. You can achieve a good status, hold influence, and so forth. So having money is basically the same as having a wish-fulfilling jewel.

The wish-fulfilling jewel will not provide happiness or provide the state of buddhahood, and neither will money. These days we consider money to be extremely important. In reality, money is just a means to bring ourselves material happiness. However, we mistakenly identify money as being the happiness itself, and it becomes our primary focus. So, in this verse, I think that realizing all sentient beings are more important than money makes it easier to comprehend the meaning of "wish-fulfilling jewel."

What is the reason sentient beings are even greater and more precious than the wish-fulfilling jewel? It is because the jewel can only bring us external wealth; it cannot develop our compassion. It cannot give us prajna. It cannot give us happiness. It cannot give us the state of buddhahood. And yet, if we treasure sentient beings and if we carry within our own being the conduct and motivation to work for the benefit of others, we will be able to develop loving kindness, compassion, prajna, the state of buddhahood, and happiness. For this reason treasuring others is more precious than owning a wish-fulfilling jewel.

Normally we place buddhas and bodhisattvas in a high place. We make offerings to them and prostrate to them. But when we see someone who is not so beautiful, perhaps wearing dirty clothes and whose face is filthy, we do everything we can to keep them away, to prevent them coming near us. But, actually, when we think about sentient beings and buddhas, we might make the analogy of clay: we can create various different shapes out of clay but the essence of clay remains the same.

If we then take that clay and make it into the shape of a buddha and put it in a high place, we will treasure it, we will make offerings to it, we will prostrate to it. If we were to take that same material and fashion it into a dog or a pig, we wouldn't do those things. The material is the same but the form is different — one is a buddha, one is a dog or a pig. If we consider the external form as being more important than the clay itself, we probably won't put dogs and pigs in high places or make offerings to them.

What this verse is saying is that in order for us to bring ourselves happiness and accomplish the state of buddhahood, we must understand there is no difference between buddhas and sentient beings; in terms of the material, the qualities, the benefits, they are one and the same. In order to achieve buddhahood, we are told that making offerings to buddhas and accomplishing benefit for sentient beings is the important thing and we consider buddhas, bodhisattvas, and gods as being most important. But we must also cherish sentient beings and recognize their qualities.

Two: Be Confident, Not Prideful

Whenever I'm in the company of others,
I will regard myself as the lowest
among all,
And from the depths of my heart
Cherish others as supreme.

This verse is actually quite difficult. Especially in these days when in our current way of looking at things, we see ourselves and others as being equal. We may not consider ourselves as being superior to others, but we do think we are equal. So when it comes to seeing ourselves as being inferior or if we don't know how to conceive of that idea, how do we train in it and practice it? It can seem to be contradictory to our present cultural norm.

The difficulty we have these days is that we often mistake confidence and pride. We get the two mixed up and often see pride as if it were confidence. For that reason we are unable to distinguish between our pride and our confidence. Confidence is something we must have, but pride is something we must give up. It is important for us to distinguish these two. Here, the text is talking about decreasing our pride by decreasing our arrogance and decreasing our tendency to ignore or think badly of others.

In general we identify pride as being something to be eliminated completely. But actually, we can distinguish two different types of pride. One is the pride to be eliminated, and the other is the pride that is an antidote. We utilize pride as the remedy when we are trying to eliminate the afflictions, because when we are struggling against the afflictions we need to believe that we can eliminate them. It is because we have been habituated to the afflictions for so long that they are very difficult to eliminate and often we will be defeated in our struggle with them. We must not engage with them, not let them get the better of us. When the afflictions arise in us, we must be able to apply the antidote, and for this reason we need to have the pride of thinking, "I am not going to let myself be overcome by them." This is confidence and is necessary, in order to know that we can disregard the afflictions, that we can override them, that we can defeat them and be victorious. So in order to overcome the afflictions we need to have the sort of pride that can diminish the afflictions; to not consider them as being important. We need to be able to say to ourselves, "I can live without the afflictions; I don't need them." We must cultivate the pride that is an antidote, in order to diminish the afflictions and finally abandon them.

But usually it is difficult for us to disregard the afflictions, to say, "I don't need the afflictions." When we are not desperate, it is not a problem, but when we are at the end of our tether, we fall back on the afflictions. If we have the power of virtue, the supporting condition, we can rise above them, but without that, we will not be able to. Without that strength of virtue, we are emptied of the positive and have no choice but to look to the afflictions for protection. So, without any virtue, we have no power, and consequently we have no choice but to rely on the afflictions. In place of that, if we do have some genuine love and compassion in our mind stream, then, only at that point, are we able to really do without the afflictions. It is only at that point we can say, "I have this precious love and compassion in my mind and I don't need you," only then will we have the confidence we can rely on and apply. But without it, we get to the end of our capacity and then it is impossible to not get attached to things that are pleasing, and angry at things that are displeasing.

The pride to be eliminated is the pride that ignores and disregards other sentient beings. It makes one look down on others and treat them with contempt. This type of pride creates big obstacles because it also closes the door to developing our own virtuous qualities. The dharma is something that requires us to improve ourselves continually in a spiritual direction, step by step. Every day we need to be just a little bit better than the previous day, and the following day a little bit better again.

We need to continually develop the qualities for ourselves, but if, on the basis of some small, limited reasoning, we were to say to ourselves, "I'm important," this would impede us from developing our qualities. This pride must be eliminated.

There are many different reasons why we can come to feel prideful: because of our social position, because we might come from a well-to-do family; because of our achievements; because of our good looks; but they all prevent us from developing our virtuous qualities. So it is important that we move in the direction of developing our own qualities.

Three: Apply the Dharma as an Antidote

In my every action, I will watch my mind,
And the moment destructive
emotions arise,
I will confront them strongly and
avert them,
Since they will hurt both me and others.

Here in English it says, "hurt." The term *nö-pa* means "causing harm" but actually, the Tibetan text reads "ma-rung-wa," which means something a little different; the meaning of *ma-rung-wa* is more like "turning you wild" or "making you rough or harsh."

No matter who they might be, in the beginning, when someone is born they are not bad in any way. But depending on that person's environment, personal situation, and their internal constitution, they can become accustomed to the afflictions as they arise, and through the force of habituation they are turned into a rough and unsavory person.

Whether we are talking about the Foundation or the Mahayana dharma, when we are talking about all of the dharma that the Buddha taught; dharma is an antidote for the afflictions and nothing else. Any person that is practicing dharma, no matter which one, whether this is the dharma of the listeners, or the Mahayana dharma, or whether it's the secret Mantrayana dharma, no matter what name you call the dharma you practice, it must all be an antidote for the afflictions. This is the critical point of the dharma; whether our dharma is functioning or not, is successful or not, comes down to this.

These practices are considered extremely important in Tibet. The reason for this is a particular feature of Tibetan Buddhism: in Tibetan Buddhism the three vehicles are practiced all together within the person of a single individual. This is considered very important. In order to practice the dharma of the three vehicles, an individual must first have practiced the three types of vows. For that reason, the three types of vows are considered a different topic and there is particular research into and teaching on them.

If, when we practice the three types of vows, three different people are practicing individually, for example: if Person A practices the pratimoksha vows of individual liberation, Person B practices the bodhisattva vow, and Person C practices the Secret Mantrayana vows, it would be simple to practice. But we don't do this, we are engaging the three practices all together.

When one individual practices all three levels at the same time, then sometimes, the vows conflict with each other. That person might come to a situation where, if they behaved according to the precepts of the pratimoksha vows it might conflict with their bodhisattva vow, or if they were to hold the practices of the Secret Mantra Vajrayana to be most important, it might contradict the pratimoksha precepts. So when these different conflicts and contradictions coexist, it becomes difficult to practice. Actually this is the area that gives the greatest difficulty to people who are practicing Buddhism.

The essence of Tibetan Buddhism is the difficult practice of the three types of vow. There has been a lot of discussion about this. For example, if we hold the pratimoksha vows, the vows of individual liberation, these are the vows of the householders — the five lay precepts and fasting vows, and the vows of male and female monastics. This discussion is not merely for the sake of being scholarly; it's primarily about how to use these as an antidote for afflictions. These vows and lay and monastic precepts are primarily antidotes to the afflictions when we work with our body and speech. We make an agreement with our body and speech not to act on desire. When we come to the bodhisattva vow, however, it's different. In fact, in some sutras the Buddha taught that for a bodhisattva, desire and attachment are not afflictions. The reason for this is that the power of the bodhisattva comes from the power of loving kindness and compassion, and attachment can be an aid in practicing the path. The problem, what is contradictory in the bodhisattva practice, which is primarily the practice of loving kindness, compassion, and bodhicitta, is our hatred and aversion. We primarily try to stop aversion and apply remedies. In the practice of the Secret Mantra Vajrayana, we do work with all the afflictions, including attachment and aversion, but the primary affliction we work with is delusion — the illusion of grasping at things as being real.

In the Secret Mantra Vajrayana, we use many different methods to prevent ourselves from clinging to things as being real. This is why there is the description of prajna and developing the wisdoms of the five buddhas and their families. This practice is primarily an antidote for delusion. And so, in summary, all the dharma becomes an antidote for the afflictions. This summarizes all three vehicles of Buddhist practice: the three vows or restraints of our body, speech, and mind.

Any dharma we practice must function as an antidote for the afflictions. The way we often do it is that we set aside a certain amount of time — a few hours, perhaps — and a particular place for practicing dharma, a shrine room. But at other times, we just let ourselves behave as usual, giving our afflictions a free rein. If we do that, then we are not really practicing the dharma: it does not become dharma practice. The text reads, "In my every action," so it has to go beyond, into whatever we are doing, not only when we are meditating in the shrine room. In order for the dharma to work as an antidote for the afflictions, we have to do it all the time, extending our practice beyond the shrine room and our formal meditation. Whatever task we're engaged with, whenever we are making a connection with other people, we need to keep this in mind. It's often said in describing the conduct of a bodhisattva that even when you fasten your belt you should check whether that action is helping to decrease the afflictions or not. Of course, that is looking at it in very fine detail, but in any case, when we are trying to overcome the afflictions, when we are practicing the dharma, if we want to have courage in the dharma, and if we want our dharma practice to be powerful, we need to look this way in all of our actions. Once we do that, we can have the confidence that we will actually be able to avert the afflictions.

We need to bring the dharma into our lives. Sometimes when we think about this, people get a little confused about it and maybe think that you have to have all the accoutrements in order to be a dharma practitioner — you need the vajra, you need the bell, you need the damaru and the skull cup, you have to take your mala everywhere you go. Sometimes this creates problems. For example, sometimes, if only one member of a single family is a Buddhist and other family members don't

have faith in any religion or have faith in a
different religion, dharma can actually become a cause of difficulties.

It can appear to others that you're being
weird about it. This is particularly a problem for Buddhists. We need to realize that
Buddhism isn't something that we have to
make a public display of. Of course, sometimes, it is just naturally visible and that is no
problem; but intentionally trying to show that
we are Buddhists does not fit with the
dharma. Actually, it becomes one of the eight
worldly concerns. When you are purposely
trying to make an impression, thinking, "Will
they be able to see that I'm a dharma practitioner?" It is actually no longer dharma practice; in fact it contradicts the dharma. When
we talk about bringing the dharma into our
lives, it means that we are able to apply the

dharma as an antidote. The dharma isn't something that we only do in the meditation room. If the afflictions only occurred when we were in the meditation room, that would be fine but that's not the way it is. Afflictions happen all the time — when we're at work, when we're trying to make connections with other people — that's when the afflictions occur. Those are the times that we need the dharma to function as the antidote and work against the afflictions.

Now when we say that you need to apply the antidotes for the afflictions such as anger, you might think this means, "I need to suppress my anger. I need to quell my anger; I need to crush it." We have a Tibetan expression that says, "Even when there's fire burning in your chest, don't let the smoke out of your mouth." You have the fire of anger burning inside but you can't show it to anyone. Actually, that's not what applying the antidote to anger means. People do think that when we say "applying the antidote" or "using the antidote" it means that you should suppress your anger, be patient, and bear with it. But when you do that, often what happens is that you are just gathering it within yourself and that's no good either, because it will only bring more suffering.

We now live in an age where people say that you need to show what you are feeling, to show what is on your mind, so when people hear, "You need to apply the antidote for the afflictions," they think that this means that you need to suppress the afflictions and deny them. But that's not what it means. When you read this line, "I will confront them strongly and avert them," there is the danger that you will misunderstand it.

That is why it suggests here that the afflictions will make us wild; we will no longer be gentle, no longer peaceful. Everyone suffers, for that reason we need to see the afflictions as being a fault. Then, when we have identified the afflictions as being a problem, at that point we become disenchanted, we feel revulsion and we feel disgust for them. When we feel disgust for the afflictions, they will naturally subside. We don't need to suppress them, there's no need to crush them, rather you identify the afflictions as being a fault and, naturally, they decrease. So this is the fundamental remedy for the afflictions.

In order to find a remedy for the afflictions, we need two different types of support:

an external support and an internal support. As an analogy, you could think about the olden days, such as in a movie about ancient times, when there were kings. There are two kings, King A and King B, and they aren't getting along so they decide to fight a war. When King A is getting ready to attack King B; if he's thinking like a general, he can only send in an army when they are ready to go into battle. So the first thing he has to think about is how to prepare for a war: he has to raise an army, train them, equip them. The second thing he must do is send spies into King B's capital city. These spies need to examine the situation: they need to see what the economy is like and how people are doing; whether the army is good or bad; what the people's attitude to King B is — do they like him? If the economy is good, the army is strong and, most importantly, if the people support and love the King, then, no matter how much war is waged, it will be difficult to win. What needs to happen is for King A to direct his spies to start spreading rumors, fomenting rebellion, creating conflict between people, influencing people to dislike King B and feel badly about him. Only at that point, when the army is attacking from the outside and there's rebellion within, when the external and internal conditions come together, can King A take the city.

It's also like that when we are applying the remedies for the afflictions. First, we need to get ready: we do prostrations; recite Vajrasattva mantras; make mandala offerings; and practice guru yoga. There are many such external preparations we need to make, including supplicating the guru. So first we prepare ourselves.

Once we feel ready to apply an antidote for the afflictions, the most important point is that if we lack complete revulsion for the afflictions in the depths of our heart and mind, then no matter how many things we do externally such as applying antidotes, gathering the accumulations, and purifying misdeeds, they won't help. They won't be remedies for the afflictions. However, if we are doing this from the depths of our heart and mind, then we will really be able to turn away from the afflictions. The main thing is that we need to be genuinely disgusted with the afflictions within our own mind. When we have that disgust and we also have the powerful external support of virtue, then it will be possible to be victorious in that battle and overcome the afflictions.

In brief, even if in the end we can overcome

everything else, we may not achieve victory over ourselves. We are our own greatest enemy; the final and most terrifying boss. This is why it is important to see the afflictions as faults when we apply the antidotes to them.

It can be difficult for us to apply the remedies. If the affliction and the remedy were separate people, it would be easy. But it's not like that: the affliction is you and the antidote is also you. So it gets confusing.

We might be trying to apply the antidotes, but if we are trying to apply them outside ourselves, it doesn't work. Actually, we have to look inside ourselves. Often, we use the afflictions deep in our mind as our closest allies: on the outside, we may have the appearance of applying a remedy, but actually, inside, we may not be really doing that, and so, for that reason it can be very complicated.

Four: Cherish the Difficult

Whenever I see ill-natured beings,
Or those overwhelmed by heavy
misdeeds or suffering,
I will cherish them as something rare,
As though I'd found a priceless treasure.

"Whenever I see ill-natured beings," ill-natured or troublesome people, it is those people for whom we particularly need to feel loving kindness and compassion. Often what happens is, when we see ill-natured or boorish people experience some mishap or suffering, we think, "It serves them right!" That's often how we feel, particularly when we see someone who has done us harm or stolen something from us and then, subsequently, their car is stolen or their house is burnt down causing injury to themselves. When we hear they are in the emergency ward we say, "Ha, they deserved it!"

That is not the practice of loving-kindness, compassion, and bodhicitta. That sort of practice is not okay. When we see a person like that, it is especially the sort of person we need to have compassion for. In fact they should be the particular focus of our compassion. It is easy to feel love and compassion for those close to us. If someone we love goes to the hospital, it is easy to have compassion for them. However, if someone who hurt us in some way is now sick or injured and is suffering, this is the moment we need to emphasize love and compassion for that person. It is at this moment that we can actually tell whether we really have loving kindness and compassion. That is the meaning of this verse. It is especially important to develop loving kindness and compassion for such people.

If it doesn't have an effect, that's fine, but if there is someone who has done you some terrible wrong, who has harmed you, and that person is now in some difficulty or pain or suffering, you should take this as a great opportunity. You should pay particular attention and interest in them and observe in yourself whether or not you have actually developed loving kindness and compassion. If you find that you have not, that's OK. But you should at least examine your mind and see. You shouldn't pretend. If, when you look to see whether you have love and compassion for that person, you find you don't, you might think, "Oh no, I'm a failure as a dharma practitioner." And then you recite, OM MANI PADME HUM and say, "Poor thing."

If that's what you do, it is actually one of the eight worldly concerns. If you try to have love and compassion and it doesn't work, that's fine, no problem. But on the other hand, if you are unable to feel love and compassion and pretend that you do, that is not the dharma. In any case, we need the chance to examine our loving-kindness and compassion in order to establish what sort of level of loving-kindness and compassion we have, and this is the perfect opportunity to do so. If we are always meditating on loving kindness and compassion but we never assess how much we have, we will never really know where we are, whether we have it or not. At this point, with that type of being and that situation, we can examine ourselves and see what degree of loving kindness and compassion we actually have.

When you write the word *buddha* forward B - U - D - D - H - A, it says "buddha," but if you write it backward, though it's still the same letters, it no longer spells buddha. Similarly, when we consider sentient beings, there can be good-natured sentient beings and bad-natured ones, and yet they both experience pain and pleasure. Just because they're bad-natured doesn't mean that they do not experience pleasure and pain. Whether good or bad natured, they are both sentient beings; they are fundamentally the same. We need to view them in this way, especially if there is some way in which we can transform a bad-natured sentient being into a good-natured sentient being. If through the power of our loving kindness or compassion, our intelligence or wisdom, we are able to make a connection and transform that being; that, I think, is acting with dignity, a truly honorable trait.

There are a lot of people out there, some people who would harm us and others who would help us. When people cause harm to us, it's natural to feel discouraged. We might hold grudges; we might feel anger and aversion. When someone is harming us, we should try to remember that that person is also experiencing feelings of pleasure and pain. If it happens not just once, but time after time, that they treat us with malice and ill-will, it is only human if we feel some discouragement and anger toward that person. But as someone who is practicing bodhicitta, loving kindness and compassion, we should try to respect that person and treat them well.

If an affliction arises when an individual harms us, that's one mistake, but if, on top of that, we also forget that they are a person who experiences pleasure and pain, and think they should not be an object for our meditation on compassion, we are doubling our mistake. The first mistake is that the affliction is arising. Then, on top of that, if we think that the harm that person causes us is more important, and their experience of pleasure and pain is less important, that whatever happens to that person serves them right, we are doubling our mistake. So, it is important for us not to double our mistakes in this way.

Five: Train to Accept Defeat

Whenever someone out of envy
Does me wrong by attacking or
belittling me,
I will take defeat on myself,
And give the victory to others.

Generally, when we practice mind training, there are two different types of practice that we do. There is the practice of meditating on the equality of self and other, and there is the practice of meditating on exchanging self and other.

When we think about the instructions on arousing bodhicitta, there are really three types. First, there are the instructions on meditating on the sequence of seven causes and results; then, there are also the instructions on meditating on the equality of self and other; and, third, the meditation on exchanging self and other.

The instructions on exchanging self and others originate in the Kadampa tradition and were initially kept secret. They were said to be a special instruction, and thus they were not taught widely or to very many people.

Later, these instructions on exchanging self and others were revealed, and, since then, they have been practiced widely.

The verse reads: "I will take defeat on myself, and give the victory to others." So, when we are training our minds in compassion for all sentient beings, there comes a point where we have such intense cherishing of and love for other sentient beings that we don't worry about how hard it is for ourselves, how bad it is for ourselves. We do not think about the difficulties we face. We are willing to give all of our happiness and everything we have to other sentient beings. So we develop much courage and conviction.

The first lines are, "Whenever someone out of envy does me wrong by attacking or belittling me." Here we are primarily discussing envy. So when someone attacks us, belittles or criticizes us, we accept the defeat and give all benefit to them. when we think about other sentient beings, when we are practicing loving kindness and compassion and someone is criticizing or belittling us, attacking us in any way, we see that person as being under the control of the afflictions. Thus what is to blame? It is not the sentient being that is to blame, but rather, blame rests with the afflictions within that sentient being. For that reason, when another sentient being attacks us, criticizes or belittles us, if we were to retaliate in return, that would neither match the way things actually are, nor would it fit with our mind training.

I think we all know this. We all understand the reasons and philosophy. But often when we have an understanding of philosophy it can remain in the head as an intellectual understanding. It's not often something that is felt really deeply in our mind and heart. So, when we come to practice it, it can be difficult, even though we understand it. An analogy would be if someone were to strike you with a stick, who would you get angry at? You would get angry at the person; you wouldn't get angry at the stick. The reason we wouldn't get angry at the stick is because the stick is not to blame. There's no fault in the stick. It's the person who uses the stick, the one who controls the stick. The stick on its own has no intention or thought to strike you. It is not under its own control. The stick has no motivation to harm you, no ill will toward you; it is under the control of someone else. And so for that reason we do not hold the stick to be at fault at all and we don't get angry at the stick. Likewise, when we think about people, they don't want to make us angry. Instead, they are under the control of the afflictions, their negative and disturbing emotions. However, when we say "emotions," I sometimes have a doubt about the use of the word. If we think about the word *emotion*, I don't know that it actually covers all of the cases of the Tibetan word *nyönmong* or the Sanskrit *klesha*. There are some afflictions that are not emotions, for example delusion. We are not even aware that delusion exists; it's not visible, so we cannot call it an emotion. Following on from that, when we are under the control of the kleshas or afflictions, what is it that is actually under their control? It is the individual. So, in this way we need to think of that individual as being controlled by the afflictions and we need to forgive them.

We should not respond to their action but

give them some space and forgiveness. So, when it says here, "I will take defeat on myself and give the victory to others." one aspect of this is that when a person is attacking and belittling us, they are under the control of the afflictions and we need to meditate on great compassion for that sentient being. In particular we should try to develop great affection and love for them because they are in an especially wretched state. For that reason, this is a situation where we really need to try to increase our compassion and increase our wish to benefit others.

For instance, if someone is set to sue you, that lawsuit itself is not something that we would meditate on compassion for. We would have to respond to the lawsuit and the court action. However, as for the individual who is suing you, if you were to get angry at them and hold a grudge against them, it would disturb your own mind and increase the afflictions. All it would do would be to make you unhappy. Whatever that individual has done is strengthened by your anger and this makes it even more uncomfortable. Actually, when we think about it, when we are being sued, if you can let your mind rest naturally while you are being sued, then you are able to think about it rationally. When you have thought about the action rationally, you can make an appropriate response. If, on the other hand, you are overcome by the afflictions, if you are not relaxed, if you are not resting naturally, whatever action you take will be mistaken or in danger of going wrong. So for that reason, we need to distinguish between the individual and their action. There are various actions and types of response possible, so we need to make the appropriate one. However, that individual is not to blame. It's not their fault. They are under the control of the afflictions. This is the situation that they are in, so we need to give them some space and it is important for us to have some compassion and understanding for the individual.

But before we are able to really develop a feeling for how it is that other individuals are controlled by their afflictions, we first need to examine the afflictions that reside within our own being and recognize them. If we do not, it will be difficult for us to comprehend the extent by which others are controlled by them and how strong they actually are.

We need the experience of how dark the blackness of ignorance actually is. We need to feel the heat of anger. We need to know all of these and understand them. It is only once we have that experience ourselves, that we can comprehend how it is that other people fall under their control.

First, in order for us to recognize the afflictions we need to use mindfulness and awareness. If we do not have mindfulness and awareness, it leads to our making mistakes through anger or delusion; how many times have we made mistakes out of anger and delusion, or desire? We have experienced these many times, and such experiences have not helped us. So it is extremely important for us to develop mindfulness and awareness.

But there are varying degrees of difficulty in recognizing the faults of the afflictions. Actually, do we know how many different afflictions there are? It is said in the scriptures that there are 84,000 afflictions. But I think that is just a figure of speech for a very large number;

it's like a plural in ancient Indian texts. You read that Indian kings had 84,000 queens. If a king had 84,000 queens, and he visited a different queen every night, there would still be more queens than he could visit in his entire lifetime. It just means there are a lot. So, there are many different afflictions, but we can summarize them into the three poisons of the afflictions.

However, some of the three poisons are easier to recognize than others.

The first one, the one that is easiest to recognize as being a fault, is anger. The second would be desire. That's a little more difficult to recognize as a fault than anger. The third one, the hardest to recognize, would be ignorance or delusion. There are also distinctions based on the relative strengths of each of the poisons within any particular individual and this can make it easier or more difficult to recognize some of the others. Although the order in general is as already mentioned; because of the distinctions between individuals and their different fortunes and dispositions, and the relative strengths of the different afflictions, some are more evident because there are more opportunities to express them.

In any case, when we discuss the faults of the afflictions, someone who has studied texts can list them and repeat them as they are written. Or maybe they will say, "The lama said this..." But this is only repeating what the lama said. Just repeating what is written in the texts or what the lama said is not enough. That is intellectual understanding, not experience. Similarly, in order to recognize the afflictions, we need to experience the faults of the afflictions in our own being. For instance, if you are talking about a person, there is a difference if you know that person compared with when you don't really know them. You can talk about them, but it's not the same as if you had really known them at first hand. If you have that direct experience, there is more depth in your understanding. Likewise, with the faults of the afflictions, there is something that we need to see and experience directly and evidently for ourselves. We need to have the experience of the afflictions through listening, contemplating, and meditation.

Recognizing the faults of our afflictions is something we need to make an effort with every day. We need to try to examine them every day to see what is their nature and how do they function? We need to use various different methods and look at them from various different angles and perspectives, which means observing them from different viewpoints. If we do not make any effort, it will be difficult to recognize them.

Right now we are talking about recognizing the faults of the afflictions, but actually if the afflictions seem to us to be one thing and their faults another, and we distinguish them as separate, then that is a sign that we haven't really completely recognized the faults of the afflictions. Actually the afflictions and their faults are inseparable. The nature of the affliction is the fault itself. They are not distinct. The affliction itself is what needs to be eliminated. It is not as if the affliction were one thing and there was some additional fault that needed to be eliminated. If we recognize that the affliction in its totality must be eliminated, that is a sign that we have truly identified the affliction.

How long will it take to recognize the afflictions? We can't really set a time frame for this. When I look at it, it seems to me that sometimes it can take five or six years or maybe ten years to recognize just one affliction. The process is long and variable. To truly recognize the fault, to recognize the affliction is something that happens in an instant. So some people are very quick about it.

When we think about our faults and recognize them as such, we see that we have them because of the afflictions in this life. When we reflect on the problems that arise in our life, this can provide a condition that aids us to recognize the faults of the afflictions. For that reason, if we think about how many different mistakes we have made, how many different faults and problems we have had, the more aware we can be of the conditions that created them. If we have the strength to be aware of those, it will be easier for us to recognize the faults. Basically, when we are thinking about a great being, they are not great because they have great qualities. They are a great person because of having overcome their faults. At first they had great problems and they overcame them; that is what is amazing. If that person from the very first had all the great qualities, there would be nothing special about their greatness. When we consider reincarnation and our past lives, we carry a mountain of faults the size of Mount Meru on our backs. With that perspective, having a few faults in this lifetime is not something that should make us discouraged or depressed. We must not be weighed down by all our misdeeds; we must be able to rise up, out from under the burden of our misdeeds. This is the method we use to turn our faults into precious jewels and generate the hope that we will be grateful that we had faults.

Six: Learn from Injustice

Even when someone I have helped,
Or in whom I have placed great hopes
Mistreats me very unjustly,
I will view that person as a true
spiritual teacher.

When there is someone whom you have helped and you have tried to do your best for, someone in whom you have great hopes, who then harms you or fools you or tricks you, that is even more discouraging, even more upsetting to us than if it were an enemy who has harmed us in any way. Yet, that sort of person is the greatest spiritual teacher for us. The reason is we need to train and develop our mind. We need to increase our compassion, and that person is pointing out and showing us where the difficulties are for us.

These days many of us live lives in cities that are busy and stressful, we have jobs, difficulties, and a lot of pressure in our lives; there are many different things that we have to do. Then, at the weekends, we go to a resort. We go to a spiritual resort and we do meditation, do some yoga, and receive some massage.

When we get there, it's wonderful and we call it practicing dharma. We wash away so much stress, it's so relaxing, and our mind feels good, our mind feels peaceful. It's very satisfying, so wonderful and so fresh. We feel great relief. But, actually, when we think about it, that's just a temporary benefit.

We often think that practicing the dharma is like that. This is not really the benefit that practicing dharma should bring, because that type of practice is like taking a pain-relieving medicine, and there are lots of pain relievers in the world. But dharma is not that type of medicine. When we talk about practicing the dharma it is an intensive training exercise. When you train intensively it takes a lot of effort, a lot of strength. There's nothing comfortable and nothing easy about it. We have to work hard. It's difficult. This is the feeling you get when you do intensive training. If you look from this perspective, at those friends who harm us, it becomes easy to see how they are the greatest of our spiritual teachers. When we are practicing the dharma it is not as easy as going for stress reduction and relaxation. This is important for us to understand.

Seven: Radiate Joy, Take on Pain

In brief, directly or indirectly,
I will offer help and happiness to all
my mothers,
And secretly take on myself
All their hurt and suffering

This verse is about the practice of exchanging ourselves with others and doing the visualization of *tonglen* or "sending and taking."

Here it says, "And secretly take on myself." From one perspective, "secretly" refers to doing it in secret. It is not that we tell the other person, "I'm taking this suffering and giving you this happiness." It is not something to show off. If we were to display it, it would become one of the eight worldly concerns. Instead, the other person should not know that we are doing the practice. For us to actually take on the suffering of another being is extremely difficult. Instead, what this means here is that we develop the motivation in our mind so that if we were able to take on the suffering of others, we would be ready to do it. Thus we develop a strong resolve to take the suffering of others on ourselves.

Many people come to me and say, "I need to do something to benefit other people so I need to be rich. I need to have a lot of money." When I hear this, I get a little suspicious about it, because if you intend to benefit others, why do you need to be rich, why do you need so much money? Then, when we talk about it, the reason given is that there are so many poor people in the world, there are so many people who have no education and if you are rich, you can provide these people with a basic livelihood or provide them with a basic education. So you need to get rich in order to benefit others. But actually, that's kind of difficult. If we were all to get rich, there wouldn't be any poor people left to help. Other people think that they need to be influential or powerful in order to be able to benefit others. But, once again, if everybody were powerful or influential, what use would power or influence be?

We think that in order to benefit others we have to be rich and powerful, but that is not the way things really are. It is not necessary to be rich and powerful in order to bring benefit.

We do not know where or who the bodhisattvas are. Until we reach the state of a bodhisattva ourselves, we can't tell who is or is not a bodhisattva. That stray dog in the street may well be a bodhisattva, but we aren't in a position to recognize them. We just don't know.

In fact, a bodhisattva is an individual, any individual, who works for the benefit of other beings. Though we can't tell who they are, they do everything they can to help us. Sometimes I feel sorry for such bodhisattvas because we don't recognize them, and since we don't recognize them as bodhisattvas, we do not feel gratitude toward them. We are real ingrates. Maybe this is actually one good thing about the Tibetan tulku system. Because of the tulku system, we are able to see this person who is recognized as a tulku as a bodhisattva. So we at least have someone we can be grateful to. Otherwise, we just wouldn't know. As well as tulkus, there are also other beings who are benefiting others without us knowing at all. Sometimes they are engaged in activities in such a way that we are not sure whether they are doing something that benefits others or does harm to them. There are many such bodhisattvas.

Really, if we are going to do something to benefit others, it has to be something we do with our body, speech, or mind. But at the moment, our body, speech, and mind are not a sufficient basis or support for us to be able to really benefit others, and so we need to gather all of the qualities of body, speech, and mind that will allow us to bring them benefit. We need to form our body into a basis with which we can benefit others. We need to make our speech into such a basis. We need to turn our mind into such a basis. We need to be able to benefit other sentient beings with our speech. We need to be able to benefit them with our mind. We need to be able to do things physically with our body that will bring benefit to other beings.

We need to be able to gather the virtuous qualities of our body, speech, and mind, because it is important for us to develop the capacity to benefit all other sentient beings. If we are able to do that, and we also happen to be rich, we will be able to benefit others. Even if we are not rich we will have the capacity to benefit them. We can be a beggar but still have the ability to help other sentient beings. We need to develop these qualities in order to really be able to bring benefit to other sentient beings without any mistake. We need to bear that in mind. If we lack that capacity, even before we had money, we might have thought, "Oh, I want to do something to help others." but then once we got the money, we found we couldn't carry it through. It's like some candidates who stand for an election. There are some, who, before the election make all sorts of promises: "I will build this road." or, "I will build these schools." But once they get elected, it's as if they've already gone beyond, passed into nonabiding nirvana, and no longer need to do anything.

Even if you were to get a lot of money, if you do not have the right intention and actions, the money may change you and influence you in a negative way.

Eight: Find Ultimate Freedom

I will learn to keep all these practices
Untainted by thoughts of the eight
worldly concerns.
May I recognize all things as like illusions,
And, without attachment, gain freedom
from bondage.

*Thus spoke the spiritual master Lang Thang
Dorje Senge. This is completed.
Sarva Mangalam.*

To paraphrase it, this verse is saying: "May we be able to do all these practices untainted by the eight worldly concerns, and may we be able to do these practices never separated from the view of emptiness — seeing all phenomena as illusion. By doing so, may we gain freedom from the bonds of samsara."

Regarding the eight worldly concerns, there are many different things that we can do to bring benefit in this life. If what we want to do is to bring benefit in this life, actually it's not necessary for us to practice the dharma. The dharma is primarily to accomplish our aims for the next life and future lives. It's not impossible that it will benefit us in this life, but primarily it's for our future lives. However, sometimes, we may not have the confidence or belief in future lives, and if we do not be-

lieve in future lives, we might think to ourselves, "What's the point? I want something
that is going to benefit me now. If it doesn't
benefit me now, I'm just not interested."

Often in the Buddhist trainings and teachings we talk about three different types of individual. The lesser individual should at a
minimum wish to free themselves from the
lower realms in their future lives. But some
texts talk about two types of lesser individual:
the individual who wants to be free of the
three lower realms in their next lifetime; and
the ordinary person who is just interested in
the needs of this life, not future lives. Even
though most texts on the stages of the path do
not focus on the ordinary lesser individual, it
seems to me that these days the ordinary individuals are more important. Thinking about

whether dharma can help us in this life has gained special importance.

The eight worldly concerns here mean primarily working to benefit yourself in this life. When we talk about the eight worldly concerns, I think the way we need to explain it is through consumerism or materialism. It's as if we all close our eyes and just shop for anything we want, buy, buy, and buy! We don't consider whether we need things or not; we just go out and buy them. You see the advertisements, sometimes the advertisement is pretty blatant and it is quite obviously a fantasy, but even so, if you see it enough times, you start thinking to yourself, "I want to be like that." I've talked about this example many times: a man on the motorcycle flying through the air. At first you see it and you are skeptical, but, if you see it enough times, the image of flying through the air with clothes and hair streaming behind captivates you. Sometimes, I even see this and think, "Wow. I'd like to be like that, I'd like to try that myself sometime."

It's as if the advertising has blinded us and we're no longer thinking or examining what we are buying. We get fixated by the ads.

On the one hand, we want to bring benefit and happiness for ourselves in this lifetime, but the advertisements and so on distract us from what is really important.

A thousand years ago, the dharma spread from India to Tibet and in Tibet they treasured it for a thousand years. They preserved and propagated it and researched into it. It's the place where the dharma has been preserved. So now, in this day, to come back to the place, which is the origin of the dharma and to be able to share the dharma with you, is, I think, a sign of the real magnificence of all of our dharma forebears. It is a sign of our great fortune. So, for that reason, I should especially like to thank all of the Indians who have come here today.

Often, I try to do as little dharma teaching and give as few empowerments and instructions as I possibly can. The reason is not because I am trying to hide anything or be secretive, but because I have very little experience and understanding. Anything I teach is little more than dry words, so I am embarrassed to speak too much. But sometimes there is really no choice, and I do have to speak a little bit and teach. So, if in my teachings, there have been any mistakes, I would like to beg your pardon for those mistakes, and I would especially like to thank all of you for coming.

Questions and Answers

—When pride manifests in the mind and we think, "I'm so good, I can do this," what is the best antidote to apply at that moment of this awareness of pride?

There is a story about this. In ancient times, there was a king who built many monasteries and stupas and supported many different sanghas. He thought to himself, "I have accumulated so much virtue; I'm so great there is no one else in the world who has such great virtue as me." Then he asked a lama, "I've done all these virtuous things. What do you think of it all?" He expected to be praised, but the lama replied, "You aren't virtuous at all."

This is how it is. When we do something virtuous and become proud of it, that destroys the virtue. We should rejoice in and appreciate the virtues we have accomplished, but it is not right to think that good acts are inevitably amazing and wonderful. It is said that we should never be content with the qualities we have achieved. You can be content with other things, but we must always think that we could do even more to improve ourselves, better our qualities, and help others. It is important to always have such an intention. This will help.

—*For those of us who are not adept at placing ourselves below others, as advised in the second*

verse, "I will regard myself as lowest among all,"
for those of us who are not good at doing this,
please advise us how in our practice we can de-
velop the habit of exchanging ourselves with oth-
ers or cherishing others more than ourselves.

With regard to placing ourselves as lowest among all, it is actually a matter of comparison. What are we comparing ourselves to? Of course, we all have our individual importance. But here it means including the infinite number of other sentient beings that exist alongside us. If we think about it, when there is someone whom you love, for whom you feel a very strong affection, you would have no hesitation to sacrifice yourself or your life in order to save that other person's life. You wouldn't even need to think about it. It's not that you yourself don't have personal value, but that you consider the other to have more value and to be of greater importance. If you don't have that strong love, and someone has to explain to you the reasons why you need to sacrifice yourself and so forth, then there's no way you are going to be able to sacrifice yourself for others, because if you lack that, no explanation would be of benefit. Here it's a question of developing that love for others to such a degree that you feel that other people's lives, other people's possessions, and other people's happiness is more important than your own. So this relates to putting others first.

During the Cultural Revolution in China there were lamas who were ordered to kill other sentient beings but they refused to do so, and because they refused, their hands were forcibly beaten with rocks. When later I spoke with some of them, they said they had no regrets. They expressed the view: "Finally my hand has had a purpose"

So it is a question of whether or not you have the capability to do this. You need to examine yourself. If you don't have such ability, there is no benefit to be got by trying. You need to examine yourself. It has to be something you are doing voluntarily. Anyway, when we say, "Regarding ourselves as the lowest," at the very least we need to see ourselves as not being better than others. It is important for us to recognize that we are all the same in experiencing feelings of pleasure and pain.

—If someone has been raped, how could the victim possibly practice love and compassion or even forgiveness? How could they not want to see the rapist suffer?

When we talk about forgiveness, or what we often call in the dharma, "forbearance"; I think many people misunderstand this. Sometimes we think that forgiving people or being patient with people means that we should let them go, let them off the hook. But it's not that. Sometimes we have to deal with things peacefully, and sometimes we have to deal with things harshly. The main thing is that we need to be patient with the afflictions. Sometimes, when someone has been victimized, when they have experienced great suffering, they keep it inside themselves. It is something that they hold in their chest, and it continues to affect them through their entire lifetime. In that case, it's the afflictions that we need to focus on. When we are able to deal with the afflictions, we will find some relief. Otherwise, if we continue to hold it within ourselves, it will be difficult to find any respite. The main thing is that we need to apply the antidotes for the afflictions, yet this is something that is also difficult to do.

—When we are dealing with the kleshas, there is a tendency to get tight and it gets more and more difficult to relax. How do we approach this in a more relaxed and spacious way?

When we are working with the afflictions or applying the antidotes for the afflictions, sometimes it is important not to take them too seriously. Otherwise, if we try to be serious, or we force things and are really tight about it, the afflictions themselves will become even more problematic. When that happens there will be nothing more that we can do. I think that we need to try to be more playful with it. Sometimes when we see the result of being too serious, what happens is we become ashamed, "Oh, it has overcome me! I have been defeated. I've lost." So we need to be like children who are playing. They aren't embarrassed about anything. They just go out and play and have fun, and they don't worry about how they look or who's to blame. We need to be playful with the afflictions, "Okay, come and get me! I'm going to fight you." We need to be a little more relaxed, more spacious about them. If we are able to do that, we can see how much we are able to deal with the afflictions, how far we can go. In general you just need to be a little more spacious and relaxed, with a more playful attitude and then it will be easier.

⌒Why does a person get afflicting emotions in the first place?

The *Treasury of Abhidharma* says that there are three causes for the afflictions to arise: not abandoning the kernels of the afflictions, the object being present, and inappropriate attention. It is because we have strong habituation to the afflictions and also because we have pleasant and unpleasant objects that are close to us. Particularly, living in cities, we see there are many different things that are either attractive or unattractive. Also the Internet and so forth bring the objects close to us. Also, we have an inappropriate attention, a wrong way of viewing things, and so, for that reason, the afflictions are more likely to arise. It is because all the causes and conditions that produce the afflictions are present that we have so many afflictions.

—*These days we have social networking, Internet discussion groups, and so forth. In these groups, there are some people who talk about their experiences of practicing the dharma and the feelings that they have. Is it okay to do this or not? Is it something that might create imprints or encourage people to practice the dharma?*

The way I think about this is that there are different types of experiences — those that we can share and those that are our own special experiences, particular to us. It seems to me fine to talk about those that are shareable, those that are common, but it is not appropriate to talk about our own particular special experiences, a result of our meditation such as a vision or a dream, for example. The reason for this is that when we tell people about our special experiences, while at first we might have a good understanding and a good viewpoint of it, later on someone else makes a response and gives a different opinion, then we might develop some doubt about it. Or, you might not be sure, or may not really have the correct understanding, and you go to a lama who has experience and has the instructions. If they say it is fine, then it's fine, and if they say it is not, then it is not. They can examine you to see whether or not you have understood. But when you go to a group like this on the Internet, anyone can say anything, and it might hinder you or prevent you from improving your practice or it might cause you to develop a wrong understanding. So, I think, it's best not to speak about your own particular special experiences or visions and so forth; it's better not to say anything about them.

⁓*What are the signs of true practice? What is the level or the mark that we need to get to, the sign we need to have to show that we have truly entered the path of practice?*

There are people who say, "Oh, my practice is going really well." And when you question them, "How is your practice going well?" They answer, "Well, I was in retreat. The food was really good. It was a nice place to stay. I was able to count all the numbers of mantras I was supposed to count. My practice is going really well." Or some people say, "Oh, my practice is going really well," and you ask them, "How is it going well?" and they say, "I'm having all these dreams. I see the Buddha's face in my dreams. I hear the words of the bodhisattvas. These are signs that my practice is going really well."

It's rare for someone to say to you, "Oh, my practice is going really well. My afflictions are decreasing and getting fewer. My pure perception, my devotion, is getting stronger." Actually, the meaning of the word dharma, the Tibetan word chos, is "to change," it's "to fix something." It's to fix or heal our wild being, to decrease the afflictions, to increase our pure perception, to increase our devotion, and to increase our bodhicitta so that they get stronger day-by-day, month-by-month, year-by-year. If that is happening, that is the sign that we are on the true path. That is how our progress in the dharma manifests. If our devotion and our pure perception decrease, if our mind grows wilder, that is the sign of the dharma not working and the practice not being effective.

—*Concerning the distinction between pride and confidence, you said that we need confidence but we have to overcome pride. I can see in my small experience that pride really stops me from improving, because I think I'm already good enough. When I feel confidence in a positive way, then I want to practice, I want to develop bodhi-citta, and so on. Now, unfortunately this is bcause of self-grasping and self-cherishing, which is a dualistic way of functioning, so it's like a roller coaster. What kind of attitude is most important to cultivate, as for instance in... slowly, slowly to leave the negative aspect and promote the good part of it?*

I think when we look at virtue, there are naturally ups-and-downs in our practice, and that is just the way that practice goes. Particularly, when we think about our emotional states. If we are in a low emotional state, our practice will often also be at a low. When we're at an emotional high, maybe our practice will be at a high. And so, in this way, in particular when we experience external difficulties, these can have a great effect on our practice. When our practice is not stable, our emotions can affect it. But I think what is important here is that our practice be continuous. We have to have confidence. We have to continue doing the practice and then, if we have trust and we practice and bring that inspiration to our practice, then, no matter what happens, it will go well. If we don't have that inspiration or belief in our practice then we will have obstacles in our practice as well.

So how is it that we should practice? Well, if we know one dharma, if we have heard one dharma teaching, we need to put it into practice right away. We need to engage while it's still fresh within us. It is important to do this.

Otherwise, if we hear a dharma teaching and we don't practice, we don't incorporate it into our being, we don't apply it to ourselves, then we hear another one, and another one — none of this is going to help us in any way.

This is a question of putting the dharma into practice and incorporating it into our being. If we listen to many different dharmas and yet we don't join them to our beings, our minds will just get wilder and wilder. So it is not really a question of how much dharma or how many different dharma teachings we have had; the question is whether we are able to really put the dharma into practice. If we can make this something we are able to do, then naturally and gradually we will develop confidence in it.

I think when we habituate ourselves to something over and over again, we naturally develop confidence, like with new types of food. At first when you are not familiar with something, you lack confidence. But you gradually develop and become confident.

It is like that with anything. When I was young and learning to speak in public, at first it was extremely difficult. My voice would get weaker than it normally was. I never usually coughed very much, but in front of a big public audience I'd start coughing a lot. Yet as I did it again and again, gradually I was able to develop the confidence and able to speak in public. It's not that I trained myself on the side, it's just that through repetition I developed the habit of doing it, and from that I developed the confidence and the ability to speak in public. I think it's the same with our practice. When we do our practice we should keep an account of it. We need to do that.

Normally, when we think about money, we keep accounts. If you have a business, you have to make a note of your profit and loss and keep a daily tally of your income and expenses. You must take an interest in it. If you just make an aspiration, "May I make a profit today," you are not going to make the profit. Success in business comes by the process of keeping track of your income and expenses and it's like this with our practice. It's difficult at first because from the very beginning we have many negative habits and many afflictions, so it's difficult for us at first to meditate. Old habits come up and we naturally fall into them again; beginning a new habit is extremely difficult.

It's like if you tell someone to relax, you say, "Relax." They immediately get tighter and more tense, especially if that person is not good at relaxing. When you tell them to relax they can't relax at all. Of course if someone's good at relaxing, they can relax. So I think that it works in this manner.

——Let us say that we are working for others, how do we deal with ourselves and others if they either don't want to be helped or they do not see your help as helpful.

This can be tricky. Sometimes when you try to help others, there are cultural differences that come into play. For example, with Asians and particularly with Tibetans, when you see an elderly person trying to get up, you rush over and try to help them. But in the case of someone from the West, when you try to help them up, sometimes they don't just refuse your help, they berate you, saying, "I can get up by myself, I can manage to do it." So, when you are trying to help others you need to think carefully about it and make sure that you are going to be able to do something of benefit. Otherwise, it's not certain whether you are going to receive thanks or a slap across the face. When we have an opportunity to help people, we need to realize that there are two different ways to do that. We can help them physically and we can also help them mentally. We might think that when we are helping others, unless we do something, which will be physically beneficial, then it won't good for them, but, actually, the primary way of benefiting others is benefiting them mentally. We can benefit others through mental ways. For example, if through our love and compassion, we are able to help someone who has a very coarse disposition to become gentler, more loving, and more compassionate, and then naturally this will bring more peace to the world and make a great contribution, so it is beneficial for ourselves as well as for others. When we practice, there are also many different methods, which is why the six paramitas are taught. We need to know all of the six paramitas, because there are different types of practices to be done at different times. We must have all of the different qualities — patience, prajna, diligence, and intelligence — all of these must be present. When we talk about benefiting others, we have to have a long view of it. It's like when talking about the stories of the bodhisattvas who were able to practice generosity that is so difficult to do, and carry out really demanding acts for a very long time, for eons. The stories talk about having enough patience to bear spending an entire eon in hell in order to benefit a single person. Whether or not that is necessary, we need to prepare our minds for the possibility.

—*Is there a method for generating bodhicitta in a very short time?*

Actually, I think, before you think about generating bodhicitta, you first have to know what bodhicitta is. Teaching and explaining what bodhicitta is would probably take a day. In any case, when we talk about generating bodhicitta, it does not arise without causes and conditions. The cause and condition for bodhicitta is great compassion, you need a compassion that encompasses all sentient beings without exception. You need to have the wish to bring all sentient beings, without exception, to freedom from suffering. That wish to free them from suffering is the compassion, but that compassion, many people say, is also not sufficient. You also need to have the extraordinary intention: the thought, "I will do it." You must have the willingness to bear that responsibility. It's easy for us to say, "I want to free all sentient beings from suffering." But that is just an aspiration. When Milarepa was discussing what bodhicitta and great compassion are like, he said that when great compassion arises from within, it is as if you are surrounded by fire. When you are encircled by fire, it is impossible to stay there. It's too hot. You do everything you can to escape the fire. Likewise, when the great compassion for all sentient beings grows from within, you feel, "I must do something about it. I have to do it. There's no way I can just sit still. I have to do something about it." Otherwise, if we were just to recite a prayer, look at it and think, "Oh, this is what bodhicitta's like," that is a little strange. We must first develop great compassion as the method for giving rise to bodhicitta.

In today's world we are bombarded by messages promoting desire and aspiration, so how do we distinguish between affliction and virtue?

Nowadays development in the world is happening very quickly. We don't have any time to think about it and we feel proud of that. Yet, when we think about it, all the people in the world, the bosses of all the large companies, the people who made Facebook, the people who made Microsoft, the boss of Apple, or any of these other companies, and if you ask them what will happen in ten years they won't be able to say. No one can tell us what's going to happen or what it's going to be like in ten years' time. Things are changing too rapidly. This is the way of these times. Things are changing so quickly that we are unable to distinguish the good from the bad. There are always new things happening, so wherever we go, both outside in the street or inside a building, we are always seeing little TV screens displaying advertisements. These days, you go into the toilet and there are advertisements in there. So we don't have the opportunity to really think or differentiate between them. This is really affecting and disturbing our minds. As a result of this, some things seem attractive to us, and then without thinking we start to feel attachment or greed, or we start feeling stingy or tight about things. This just naturally happens. For this reason, I think, we are unable to distinguish what we need from what we want.

We confuse these two. If we can use this as an analogy for virtue and nonvirtue, what we need can be seen as virtue, wanting corresponds to nonvirtue. When we need something we have to identify it, we have to think about it. We have to examine it. We have to ask, "Do I really need this? Is there a reason for me to have it?" With wants, we don't look for a reason. Just wanting it is enough. "I want that. I desire that." That alone is enough for us to act and we don't need any other reason.

When we recognize a need, we have control over our minds, it correlates with when we have virtue. When we are afflicted, that takes control of our mind away from ourselves. Virtue is what gives us the control of our mind, and yet, when an unvirtuous cognition, an unvirtuous mind manifests, then we have no flexibility or control over it. So I think we can consider it like this, "Is this a moment when I have control over my mind, or not?" If we can have that control over our mind we can also have a little bit of space to be able to distinguish what it is that we should engage with, and what it is that we should give up.

Glossary

AFFLICTIONS: The mental events of desire, aversion, ignorance, pride, wrong view, envy, and so forth that motivate harmful actions that perpetuate samsaric suffering.

BODHICITTA: The wish to achieve buddhahood in order to bring all sentient beings to perfect enlightenment.

BODHISATTVA: A person who has roused bodhicitta and taken the vow to achieve buddhahood for the sake of all beings. In common usage, this refers especially to those who have developed realization of the nature of truth.

BODHISATTVA VOW: The vow to bring all beings to enlightenment.

BUDDHAHOOD: The state of complete enlightenment, in which all the obscurations have been removed and wisdom is fully developed.

DAMARU: A small, two-headed hand-drum used in Vajrayana rituals.

EIGHT WORLDLY CONCERNS: Feeling happy about gain, fame, praise, and pleasure and unhappy about loss, obscurity, criticism, and pain.

FIVE BUDDHAS AND FIVE FAMILIES: The five buddhas and their families are each associated with the purification of particular aggregates and afflictions and the five wisdoms that arise from that purification.

FOUNDATION VEHICLE (HINAYANA): The initial teachings given by the Buddha to his disciples that emphasize the importance of self-discipline and teach the lack of an individual self.

GURU YOGA: One of the four uncommon preliminary practices. It involves supplicating the guru in order to receive their blessings and develop realization swiftly.

KADAMPA SCHOOL: A lineage that sought to restore the pure teachings of Buddhism that originated in the eleventh century.

LISTENERS: The shravakas, or disciples of the Buddha who follow the teachings of the

Foundation vehicle with the goal of nirvana and freedom from samsara.

MAHAYANA: The second set of teachings given by the Buddha, which emphasize teachings on compassion, bodhicitta, and the selflessness of all phenomena.

MALA: A string or rosary of 108 prayer beads.

MANDALA OFFERING: The third of the four uncommon preliminary practices, in which one imagines offering the entire universe as a way to gather merit.

NAGAS: Water serpents and otherworldly beings that dwell in caves.

PARAMITAS: The six transcendences of generosity, discipline, patience, diligence, meditation, and wisdom. They are so called because they transcend ordinary, worldly generosity and so forth.

PRAJNA: The discernment that distinguishes what is dharma from what is not.

PRATIMOKSHA: Vows such as the monastic vows and lay precepts that primarily involve committing to refrain from harmful actions of body and speech.

PRATYEKABUDDHAS: Literally the "self-awakened." Individuals who achieve nirvana in their final lifetime on their own, without relying on a spiritual teacher.

SAMSARA: The never-ending cycle of birth-death-rebirth driven by the afflictions, especially ignorance and craving.

SECRET MANTRA: Another name for Vajrayana.

SEVEN CAUSES AND RESULTS: The contemplations for generating bodhicitta:
1. Recognizing all sentient beings as our mother; 2. Recognizing our mother's kindness; 3. Returning her kindness; 4. Affectionate love; 5. Great compassion; 6. Extraordinary intention, and 7. Bodhicitta.

SKULL CUP: The upper portion of a human skull used in some Vajrayana practices.

THREE POISONS: Greed, hatred, and delusion, which are the basis from which all other afflictions develop.

TONGLEN: The practice of visualizing giving away all your merit and happiness and taking in all the suffering of others in order to decrease your cherishing of yourself and increase your cherishing of others.

TREASURY OF ABHIDHARMA, the: One of the five great texts of Buddhist philosophy. Written by Vasubandhu in the fourth century, it presents the Foundation vehicle teachings on Buddhist phenomenology.

TULKU: A lama, especially in Tibet, recognized as the reincarnation of his predecessor.

VAJRASATTVA PRACTICE: The second of the four uncommon preliminaries, which purifies misdeeds and obscurations.

VAJRAYANA: The highest or swift vehicle that includes practices for training the mind using visualization, mantra, and other techniques.

Acknowledgments

First and foremost we would like to thank our precious guru, Gyalwang Karmapa, for offering these wonderful teachings and allowing us to publish them. His Holiness also made the "Nyingje" (Compassion) calligraphy featured on the cover of this book.

His teachings were translated live by Khenpo David Karma Choephel and then Jo Gibson took the task of transcribing them from the recordings made by Gyalwang Karmapa's webcast team. The transcript was later checked against Tibetan by Maria Vasilieva and throughly edited by Annie Dibble. Final proofreading was done by Maureen McNicholas, who prepared the book to be published by KTD Publications. Beata Stepien coordinated and designed the cover and the eBooks. We would like to thank everyone involved and also Dharma Treasure for their cooperation and support.

The root translation used in the teaching and presented here was prepared by Rigpa Translations and published on the Lotsawa House website.* We would like to thank them for making the text freely available to all.

May it bring lasting happiness!

*https://www.lotsawahouse.org/tibetan-masters/geshe-langri-thangpa/eight-verses-training-mind

Published by
KTD Publications and Dharma Ebooks
KTD Publications
335 Meads Mountain Road
Woodstock, New York
E-Book published by DHARMAEBOOK.ORG
Dharma Ebooks is a project of Dharma Treasure,
which operates under the editorial guidance of
the 17th Karmapa Ogyen Trinley Dorje

© 2020 by the 17th Gyalwang Karmapa, Ogyen
Trinley Dorje
Translation by Khenpo David Karma Choephel
Root text translation: Rigpa Translations
(Lotsawa House)
"Nyingje" calligraphy by the 17th Gyalwang
Karmapa
ISBN: 978-1-934608-59-3
Printed in the USA on PCR, acid-free paper